W9-CJG-739

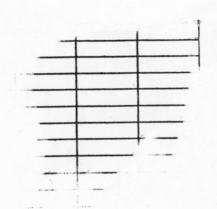

A New True Book

MEXICO

By Karen Jacobsen

*This "true book" was prepared
under the direction of
Illa Podendorf,
formerly with the Laboratory School,
University of Chicago*

CHILDRENS PRESS, CHICAGO

Mexican folk art

PHOTO CREDITS

Mexican Government Tourism Office—cover, 2, 14, 24 (top), 30 (left), 44 (bottom)

Colour Library International—4, 13 (left), 23 (2 photos), 26, 29, 42 (top), 44 (top, middle)

A. Kerstitch—8, 9 (2 photos), 15, 27 (2 photos), 34, 38 (bottom), 45

Eugenia Fawcett—10, 12, 16, 17, 19, 20, 22, 24, (bottom), 25, 30 (right), 32, 36, 39, 40, 42 (bottom)

Shell Oil Company—38 (middle)

Volkswagen de Mexico—38 (top)

Cover—Young girl at a fiesta

Library of Congress Cataloging in Publication Data

Jacobsen, Karen.
  Mexico.

  (A New true book)
  Includes index.
  Summary: Discusses the geography and history of Mexico as well as the ways of life of its people.
  1. Mexico—Juvenile literature. [1. Mexico]
I. Title.
F1208.5.J3   972   82-4437
ISBN 0-516-01632-6   AACR2

580357
8268

TABLE OF CONTENTS

Puerto Vallarta

THE LAND

What do you know about Mexico? Are these sentences true or false?

1. Mexico has mountains.
2. Mexico has jungles.
3. Mexico has deserts.
4. Mexico is hot.
5. Mexico is cool.

These sentences are all true! In Mexico you will find all these things—and much more!

Mexico is part of the continent of North America.

Its neighbor to the north is the United States of America.

Its neighbors to the south are Guatemala and Belize.

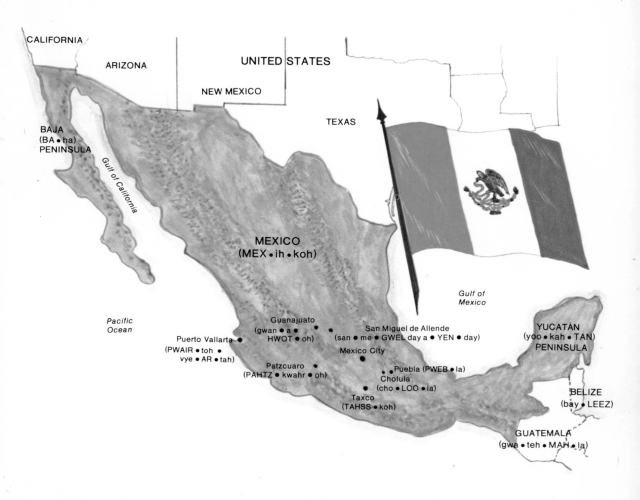

The Pacific Ocean is
west of Mexico. The Gulf
of Mexico is east.

7

Mexico has two large peninsulas. A peninsula is a piece of land that has water on three sides.

The Yucatán Peninsula forms the eastern end of Mexico. There are jungles on the Yucatán Peninsula.

Jungles of the Yucatán Peninsula

Cactus on the desert (left) and quiet
sea coves (above) are both features of
the Baja Peninsula.

The Baja California
Peninsula is on Mexico's
western coast. "The Baja"
is almost 800 miles long.
It is one of the longest
peninsulas in the world.

The Baja has high
mountains and dry, desert
areas.

Two volcanoes southeast of Mexico City

There are three mountain ranges in Mexico. Together they form a giant "V." The mountains run down one side of the country and back up the other side.

All three mountain ranges are named "Sierra Madre." Sierra means mountain range.

Between the mountains lies the large and wide plateau. In some places it is flat. In other places it is very hilly.

Much of this land has very little rain, so it is usually very dry.

Prickly pear cactus

Left: San Miguel
Above: City of Guanajuato

THE PEOPLE OF MEXICO

Today many people in Mexico live in cities and towns.

They work in offices and factories.

HOMES

Many Mexicans live in
modern houses and
apartments.

But not all the people
live in big cities.

In many villages, people live the same way that people have lived for hundreds of years. There are very few changes.

In the jungles, Indians build their houses from bamboo trees and palm leaves.

Bamboo and palm leaf house in Yucatán

Adobe houses in Santa Cruz de las Huertas (SAN • ta CROOZ DAY LAHSS HWAIR • tass)

In hot, dry places, many Mexicans use "adobe" to build their houses.

This adobe house is covered with stucco. The pottery deer on the roof lets people know that a potter lives here. It is like a sign without words.

Adobe is a mixture of wet clay and straw. It dries hard like cement.

On hot days, adobe walls hold cooler temperatures inside the house.

FOOD

For thousands of years corn has been the most important food in Mexico.

The Indians were the first corn farmers. They planted corn in the spring and harvested it in the fall.

After the harvest, they dried the corn under the sun. Dried corn will keep for a long time.

Husks of corn are often stored in branches of trees or cacti. These husks are used for cattle feed.

Corn is a part of almost every Mexican meal. It can be served as a vegetable or cooked in a stew.

But the main use of corn is to make "tortillas." Tortillas are flat cakes that are baked on a hot pan.

Tortillas can be eaten plain or filled with meat or vegetables.

Another favorite food in Mexico is "frijoles." Frijoles are beans that are boiled and mashed and then fried in fat.

Most Mexican food is made or served with hot, red chili peppers.

Chili peppers are spread out to dry in the sun.

CLOTHES

In the cities of Mexico most people dress as we dress.

But in the country, many people wear different clothing.

Mexican men usually wear white cotton shirts and pants. To protect themselves from the sun and the rain, they wear wide-brimmed hats, called "sombreros."

The sombero (above) and serapes (right), are traditional Mexican clothes.

For warmth, they might wear a wool blanket, called a "serape." Most serapes are handwoven and their colorful patterns are very old.

Mexican women usually wear cotton skirts and blouses. Often their clothes are decorated with beautiful embroidery.

Women in Pátzcuaro wear the rebozo.

A long shawl, called a "rebozo," can be used for warmth and as protection from the sun. A rebozo can also be used to carry packages and small children.

Food (above) and sugar cane (below) are sold on market day.

Woman selling baskets

Once a week in villages all over Mexico there is a market day. The people come to buy or sell food and many other things.

On market day people have a chance to visit with friends.

Indians from the northern part of the state of Oaxaca weaving in a square in Oaxaca

THE INDIANS IN MEXICO

Most Mexican people are part Spanish and part Indian.

Spanish is the official language in Mexico. But many Indians still speak their own languages.

For thousands of years the Indians were the only people in Mexico. They planted crops and raised turkeys for food. They wove cotton and made clay pots and statues. They carved stone and built huge buildings.

The Olmec Indians were strong and smart.

The Indians made clay pots and statues.

They carved huge stone statues, shaped like heads. They designed and used a calendar. They had a counting system, too.

Once the Maya Indians had a large empire. They built big, beautiful stone temples to worship their gods.

They also had a kind of picture writing. It was used to record important dates and events.

Pyramid of the Moon

The Maya were important
for 600 years.

Above: Aztec (AZ • tek) calendar stone
Right: In the 1600s the Spanish built this
Catholic Church on top of the Aztec
Pyramid at Cholula.

Later, the Aztec Indians became the most important tribe in Mexico. The Aztecs ruled other tribes in southern Mexico.
The Aztecs owned a huge treasure of gold and jewels.

THE SPANISH IN MEXICO

Montezuma was the Aztec emperor when the Spanish came in November, 1519. The Spanish army was led by Hernando Cortez. His army had sixteen horses and several cannon.

Indian dancer performs a traditional dance

The Indians had never seen white men, horses, or cannon before. They thought that the Spaniards were gods.

At first the Aztec welcomed the Spaniards. But soon they realized that the Spanish only wanted to take their gold.

In June of 1520 fighting began. Montezuma was murdered. But the Aztecs drove Cortez and the Spaniards out of their city.

The Spaniards came back. Cortez and his men took over the Aztec empire in 1521. They named it New Spain.

This church at Taxco was built more than 450 years ago.

New Spain covered all of Mexico and part of what is now the United States.

The Spanish brought their language, their government, and their religion with them. Old Spain was a Roman Catholic country, and New Spain became one, too. Old Spain ruled New Spain for three hundred years.

Statue of
Miguel
Hidalgo
(me • GWEL
ee • DAHL • go)

In 1810 Miguel Hidalgo
called for freedom. The
War of Independence
began.

Mexico became independent in 1821. It was a very large country.

Mexico went through many changes. But its leaders and its people were never again ruled by Old Spain.

Above: Volkswagen
assembly plant
Right: Drilling
for oil
Below: Trawler
unloading shrimp

Famous Talavera (ta • la • VAIR • uh) pottery, Puebla

MEXICO TODAY

Today, Mexico makes and sells oil, steel, cement, automobiles, paper, and many other things. The growth of industry in Mexico means that more and more Mexicans can earn a good living.

Education is very
important in modern
Mexico.
There are public schools
for all Mexican children
and adults.

Church square, San Miguel de Allende

Children go to at least six years of elementary school. Some students go on to a five-year high school. Many students go to three-year schools. Here students learn the skills that are needed for jobs.

Each year more and more students graduate from Mexico's schools and universities.

Carnival in Muna, (MOON • ya) Yucatán Peninsula

Feast of Virgin of Zapopan (sah • POH • pahn)

In Mexico holidays are very special. There are *fiestas* (festivals). There are special foods to eat and lots of music and dancing.

One of the most popular holidays is Independence Day. It is celebrated on September 16. This day marks the beginning of Miguel Hidalgo's War of Independence in 1810.

Butterfly net fishing
on Lake Pátzcuaro

Aztec Stadium,
Mexico City

Xochimilco
(so • chee • MEEL • koh),
the floating
gardens, Mexico
City

Beach in Sonora

Mexico has always been a beautiful country. Today, it is also a strong country. The future looks bright for Mexico. Today, more than ever, the people of Mexico have a lot to celebrate.

WORDS YOU SHOULD KNOW

adobe(ah • DOH • bee) —a sun-dried clay brick.

bamboo(bam • BOO) —a tall grass that looks like a tree that grows in warm places.

brim —the part of a hat that stands out from the crown or center.

carve —to form an object by cutting into a solid material.

celebrate(SELL • ih • brait) —to praise or show honor.

continent(CON • tih • nent) —one of the seven main landmasses of earth.

decorate(DEK • or • ate) —to add something that will make an object look better or beautiful.

desert(DEZ • ert) —a hot, dry area usually covered with sand.

embroider(em • BROY • der) —to sew fancy designs on cloth.

empire(EM • pyre) —a group of countries under one ruler.

fiesta(fee • ESS • tah) —a festival or celebration.

frijoles(free • HOLE • eez) —beans that are boiled, mashed, and then fried.

harvest(HAR • vest) —to gather in the crops.

huge(HYOOJ) —very big.

important(im • POR • tent) —to have great meaning or value.

independent(in • dih • PEN • dent) —not controlled by other people.

industry(IN • duss • tree) —to make things by businesses and factories.

market(MAR • ket) —a public place to buy and sell goods.

modern(MOD • ern) —being up-to-date; recent.

official(oh • FISH • il) —approved; proper.

palm(PAHM) —a kind of tree that grows in warm parts of the world.

peninsula(pen • IN • SOO • lah) — a piece of land that is almost surrounded by water and connected to a larger body of land.

plateau(PLAT • oh) — a flat area that is higher than the land around it.

produce(pro • DOOSS) — to make or build something.

range(RAYNJ) — a group of mountains.

rebozo(rih • BO • zoh) — a long shawl worn by people in Mexico.

rule(ROOL) — to control or govern.

serape(sir • RAH • pee) — a wool blanket worn by people of Mexico.

sombrero(som • BRARE • oh) — a wide-brimmed hat.

statue(STAT • choo) — a likeness of something or someone carved out of a solid material.

tortilla(tor • TEE • ya) — a round, flat Mexican bread made from cornmeal and water.

treasure(TREJ • er) — a collection of valuable things.

university(yoon • ih • VER • sity) — a school that is made up of colleges.

worship(WER • ship) — to honor; to show respect.

INDEX

About the Author

Karen Jacobsen is a graduate of the University of Connecticut and Syracuse University. She has been a teacher and is a writer. She likes to find out about interesting subjects and then write about them.